L

is for

Love

Magick

Kitchen Table Magick Series

by
G. Alan Joel

Esoteric School of Shamanism & Magic

Email: *alan@shamanschool.com*
Website: *www.shamanschool.com*

Publisher: Esoteric School of Shamanism and Magic, Inc.

Disclaimer and Legal Notice:
The Esoteric School of Shamanism and Magic has made every effort to ensure, at the time of this writing, that the information contained in this book is as accurate as possible. The publisher and author make no warranties or representation with respect to the completeness, fitness, accuracy, applicability, or appropriateness of this book's contents. This book's information is provided strictly for entertainment and educational purposes. Should you choose to use or apply the ideas provided in this book, you take full responsibility for your own actions. The publisher and author provide no guarantee that your life will improve in any way should you choose to use the information presented in this book. The ability of the information provided in this book to provide self-help and life improvement to the reader is entirely dependent upon the reader. The reader's ability to gain positive results from the information presented in this book is entirely dependent on the amount of time the reader devotes to the application of the material in this book, the willingness of the reader to dedicate time and effort to learning the materials presented in this book, as well as the reader's own belief system, which may help or hinder the reader's ability to benefit from this book's materials. Since each reader differs according to willingness and openness to the information available in this book, the author and publisher cannot guarantee success or improvement for every individual reader. Neither the publisher nor the author assumes responsibility for the reader's actions, or whether the information is used for negative or positive purposes. The information contained in this book is drawn from tribal traditions—both modern and ancient—as well as the author's 30 plus years' experience researching and teaching this material to students. The information in this book is presented as interpreted by the author, and, as such, may or may not be entirely accurate. In no way should the information presented in this book be a substitute for advice from health or mental health professionals.

[this page intentionally left blank]

Love Magick Blessing

Child of Wonder
Child of Flame
Nourish My Spirit and
Protect My Aim.

What I seek is love
Which the Angels can bring from high above.
A partner, a soul mate, a friend I can trust
These characteristic of my love be truly a must.

To be in love with love and all that the Spirit of Love can
bring
This fulfillment and joy I seek be so perfect that my heart
doth sing!
As I do the rituals offered in the material here
My heart will remain open and free from all fear.

These rituals send my wishes to beings of the higher
So, such beings can deliver me the perfect love I desire.
Tried and true be these workings of magick and miracles
That with faith and trust I may walk this path so spiritual.

Thus my will, so mote it be!

Free Gift

To thank you for purchasing this book, I'd like to give you a

100% FREE GIFT

Learn more about your free magickal gift.

Access Your Free Gift at
www.shamanschool.com

Find a complete list of magickal resources on https://amzn.to/3swxvPo. These resources are constantly updated so check back often!

Kitchen Table Love Magick
Table of Contents

[this page intentionally left blank]

Introduction to Kitchen Table Love Magick

We're asking you to trust in the Well-being. In optimism there is magic.
~Abraham

A Note About This Introduction

This book is one of a series of books in the Kitchen Table Magick series. Each book in the series addresses a specific area of magick (love, money, psychic development, etc.), and is written in a simple "recipe" format for people who want to use magick in their lives immediately. The Kitchen Table Magick series is akin to a Julia Childs recipe book, only these books contain magickal recipes for people to cook up some miraculous and magickal manifestations in their lives.

Because this series was designed so that each person could pick and choose to read just the books that pertain to their current life situation, each book is meant to be readable as a stand-alone book. To introduce the new reader to the series, this introduction to the series is repeated at the beginning of each book. If you have already read one or more books in this series, please feel free to jump ahead to the recipes that interest you. At the same time, some people feel that reviewing the introduction, as well as the "Rules and Tips," is helpful before diving in. In magickal circles, your will is the guideline so choose whichever route best suits you... the Universe and magickal beings will follow!

1

What is Magick?

Many people have multiple different ideas about what magick is or can be. For the sake of clarity, here is what we know about magick after more than 35 years of study and practice. Magick is a precision science! It is also:

- The science of deliberate creation.
- The science of effective prayer.
- The science of manifesting Higher Will (substitute whatever Higher Force is most familiar to you) on the energetic and material planes.
- The science of heightened awareness, selective perception, and dynamic, harmonious relationships.
- The study of intention (as per Aleister Crowley, one of the greatest magickal practitioners in history).
- The system of creation, not coercion. Note: The word manipulation is often used in conjunction with magick, but manipulation simply means the use of the hands. It should be an "OK" word without a lot of charge, but currently it is used mostly to mean coercion. Look it up!
- The principle that every intentional act is a magickal act! Magic gives us the ability to communicate with beings on all levels, and allows us to understand, through direct experience, the actual workings of the Universe.
- The traditional path of spiritual growth.
- Not extraordinary knowledge. It is the "normal" way of life. We've just lost access to it. When you have this kind of knowledge in your understanding, you have the ability to resolve spiritual questions that otherwise become catechism. From a magickal point of view, catechism is not acceptable, since a practitioner must experience and verify everything for him or herself. It avoids the trap of dogma. In past times, having a magickal foundation was essential so that we could talk directly to higher beings in the Universal hierarchy.
- Necessary to effective religious practice.

There is some confusion as to how to spell the word "magick." There are three different commonly used spellings: magick, magic, and majick. Eliphas Levi first used the form "magick" to differentiate religious or ceremonial from stage magick. All forms of spelling are acceptable in what this author teaches.

"I love Kitchen Table Magick! It's the best mix of both mystical and down-to-earth magick I have ever encountered. The fact that I can use items from my pantry is so handy and fun! It literally is about cooking up magic at my kitchen table, and having love show up in the least expected places!"
~Wendy J., Skokie, IL

Is Magick Real?

Yes. Magic is very real and has existed as a precise science for thousands of years. Whether you use the word magick or another name, this spiritual practice is very real. Every single person can learn to do magick. We are ALL born with the talents and abilities that empower us to do magick. The only reason that magick seems so, well, magickal is that this society no longer teaches the art and science of magick. In the distant past, magickal study was just as important as math, science, or the arts. In fact, magick was and still is the birthright of EVERY planetary citizen.

Can you learn to do the kind of magick portrayed in the movies? Yes... and no. The movies are great at giving you a taste of what you can do with magick, but they are not very accurate. In the Harry Potter movies, for instance, the characters use their Wands for every magickal operation. In reality, you can only use the Wand to handle Air energies. Your Wand would actually explode or catch fire if you tried to use it to throw Firebolts and Fireballs as the characters do in the movie.

So, what can you actually do with magick? Quite a lot. Here is a short list to get you started:

- Balance your energies for healing and manifestation
- Change old beliefs
- Defend yourself against physical and psychic attack
- Heal yourself and others
- Find hidden information and see possible futures (and change the future if you do not like the probable futures you divine)
- Psychically communicate with other beings
- Create sacred space
- Find lost people and objects
- Manifest what you want and need in life

At the very basis of magick is the understanding of the four elements: Air, Fire, Water, and Earth. Called elemental magick, these foundational elements are real. Air, Fire, Water and Earth are part of our natural everyday environment. What makes them magickal is the understanding of how they operate not just on the physical level, but also at the levels of Mind and Spirit.

For instance, while on the physical level Air is just the stuff we breathe, on the magickal levels Air is the conduit of psychic communication, enlightenment, understanding, dreaming, and more. If you want more of any of these things in your life, then you need more magickal Air. How do you get more magickal Air? Wear more Air colors, including white for communication and sky blue for enlightenment and understanding. To take this one step further, you could also use various magickal techniques to take on more Air to make your body lighter. Take on enough Air and you'll be able to levitate.

By just extending your understanding and use of the basic ingredients of nature, you are doing magick! Seen in this light, magick isn't all smoke and mirrors, nor is it the result of Hollywood special effects. Magic is the result of truly understanding and working with the very elements that are all around you.

One final note: Many masters, including Wayne Dyer, have said, "You'll see it when you believe it." The same is true for magick. In other words, the suspension of disbelief and the willingness not to exercise contempt prior to investigation are requirements for magick to be "real." Magick is all around us, and always is, but our ability to perceive and use the forces of magick depends on our willingness to be open. No one else can show it to you, only your direct experience and observation can "prove" or demonstrate to you that magick is real.

What is Kitchen Table Magick?

Kitchen Table Magick is exactly what it sounds like—a series of simple recipes that you can literally "cook up" at your kitchen table using household ingredients from your own pantry and cupboard.

The Kitchen Table Magic books have been created for ordinary people who want to mix up a little magick in their lives without all the fancy rituals, but simply with everyday ingredients that can be found in the kitchen pantry, bathroom medicine cabinet, or even stuffed in the back of the junk drawer.

The goal of these books is to allow anyone with the desire to learn this craft to mix up magick literally at the kitchen table using simple recipes. What goes into a simple recipe?

- Everyday items as ingredients
- Easy to follow instructions that don't require years of training
- Procedures that take less than two hours from start to finish
- Built-in expertise that allows the magick to do the heavy lifting
- Some friendly advice on how you can help your magickal recipe provide the best results
- Oh, and a few little rules and guidelines about magickal practice in this specific arena that will keep you safe and sound, magickally speaking, when you use these recipes

6

Kitchen Table Magick Equals:
Quick – Effective – Safe – Everyday Use – Ordinary
Affordable Ingredients

Why Use Kitchen Table Magic?
- Everyone can do magick
- Magick should be simple, effective, and start working right away, else it is not magick
- Not everyone has the time or resources to enroll in a school
- People ask us for magickal help in hundreds of emails everyday... Kitchen Table Magick is designed to help these very people.
- Of the many areas of life, most people only seem to need help in one or two areas, so you need only buy those Kitchen Table Magick books that apply to your needs
- Magic is for the masses, and should be accessible, affordable, and simple to do. This is what our teacher taught us, and this is the legacy we are paying forward as well
- While there are many more advanced forms of magick, these books are an introduction to that world so that you can dabble, experiment, try things out, see the result, adjust and amend, and generally have fun... just as you would cooking a meal in your kitchen.
- This book is not for the major foodie, but is perfect for the person who needs magickal help right here, right now!

Who Should Use These Recipes?
- You and anyone you know who would like a little more magick and a little less ordinary reality in their lives.
- Anyone who needs help RIGHT now and doesn't have time to fly to India or Sedona to sit at the feet of a guru.

Anyone who does not have access to anything but a computer for help and guidance.
- Anyone who wants to do magick and then forget it (all while quietly watching the magick "do its thing").
- Anyone who wants affordable, down to earth magick they can do with regular ingredients in the comfort of home.

When to Use Kitchen Table Magic: Anytime...

- You need help.
- You don't want to do all the heavy lifting (leave that to the angels, Spirit guides, animal totems, and so forth).
- You seem stuck in a rut or corner with no way out.
- You've been struggling with a problem for a long time and need a resolution.
- You don't know what to do but you need to do SOMETHING.
- You'd like to learn how to practice the craft.
- You want to live a more magickal life and stop dealing with ordinary hassles all the time.

How Do We Know These Recipes Work?

- We teach a slew of these recipes in one-day workshops all over the country, via teleconference, and via videoconference. We also email them to people as part of our school's service work, or post them on our blogs and articles library.
- We have used them for over 35 years and still do every single day – literally tested out at our own kitchen tables for over 35 years, and at thousands of kitchen tables around the world for a quarter century or more
- We receive all kinds of stories and testimonials from happy successful students. Read the following example to discover how Love Magick works in real life...

Kitchen Table Love Magick at Work...

We receive all kinds of stories and testimonials from happy successful students. Read the example below to discover how Love Magick works in real life...

Making Room for Love

After reading a blog post on the Esoteric School of Shamanism and Magic website, I was totally inspired to change my life. Specifically, I was moved to change my life to make more room for love. The blog post talked about the different ways people could make room in their lives for the sacred, and I decided the same was true for any aspect of life, from love to financial freedom to joy and more.

While I had already been making room for love by changing the way I viewed other people--by being less negative about certain people in my life and opting for a more social persona--the blog post inspired me to think about other ways to create space in my life for love.

One area that really got my attention was physical space. While I was already working on making mental and emotional room for love in my life, when I looked around my house, I could see that I had not made any physical room for love. While my house would not fall into the "hoarder" category, I had definitely accumulated some messy clutter through ten years as a single woman. There definitely wasn't any free and open space for the man of my dreams to store clothing or personal items or anything else that comes with a soul mate.

I decided to tackle this problem with a series of garage sales. I figured that if I posted the dates of my garage sales in the paper and online, I would be forced to go through the clutter in different rooms of my house. I chose the dates for four garage sales, each two weeks apart. I assigned myself the task of cleaning out two rooms of house for each garage sale. For instance, for the first garage sale I would sell the clutter and excess from my master bedroom and bath, plus the guest room. The second garage sale would feature items from my office and living/dining room.

Once the dates were posted, I was totally wired for action. I tackled the job of cleaning out clutter with zest after work and on weekends. As I cleaned, I also reorganized the remaining items with an eye towards my new potential soul mate. I set aside empty dresser drawers, an empty shelf in my medicine cabinet, and two drawers in my office file cabinet. I made room in the garage for another car. Spices and other culinary wonders were tossed out of the pantry to create an empty shelf for my new soul mate's favorite cooking ingredients.

I had attempted to clean out my house in the past with very little success. The task seemed overwhelming. But when I tackled this job with an eye toward making room in my life for love, I was so inspired that I cleaned out my assigned rooms with an abundance of energy. I was happy to toss all kinds of possessions to make room for a masculine companion in my life.

So, what happened? Nothing much. I was a little disappointed when I had finished my fourth garage sale and no new love interest had appeared in my life. I thought that I might meet an interesting man at one of my garage sales or while I was donating tons of items to the local charity. Not so. A few weeks went by with no action. One day I stopped by our local bakery to get myself a "sweet treat" as solace, since I had made a tremendous effort to make room for love in my life, yet no love had shown up. I was a little depressed and blue.

As I was browsing through the bakery's many chocolate and frosted items, I heard a man talking to one of the employees at the other end of the bakery. He was looking for an appropriate dessert to bring to a potluck, specifically, the potluck hosted by my neighbors. The bakery employee, a long-time friend of mine, pointed the man in my direction, telling him that I was also going to the potluck and probably had some ideas of what to bring... Hmmm...

To make a long story short, my "sweet treat" that day turned out to be a new leading man in my life rather than a puff pastry. Suffice to say, love is sweeter than any puff pastry. On balance, I would also say that the effort of cleaning out my house over a two-month period was more than worth it. The results took a while to manifest, but the Universe delivered the perfect person into my life. And we were able to easily integrate our lives, not only because he was a perfect fit for me, but also because there was lots of extra room in my house for my new love to move in.

The moral of this story? If you feel like you need to "do something" to speed up the process of manifestation, try making some physical space for whatever it is you want. In my case, emptying out some drawers and shelves and rooms was the way to open my life to new love. Ready for a new career? Try boxing up and storing the paper and "stuff" associated with your old or current career. Make room in your wardrobe for the right kinds of clothes for your new career. Make room in your social network for new people who have the right connections to help you start your new career. See how the strategy of physical action to attract the new can work in your life? I know I have used it many times now on different aspects of my life with really fun and interesting results. Your creativity is the only limit to what you can bring into your life!

~ Joan B., Baltimore, MD

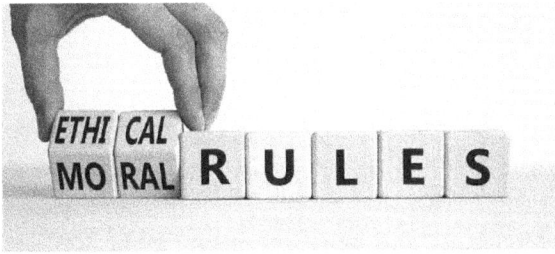

A Few Rules and Tips About Kitchen Table Magick

As with any game, the game of life has its own set of rules. Specifically, the spiritual side of life has rules. Play by those rules and you will stay safe and easily attract what you want into your life. Break those rules and all types of unwanted consequences happen.

These "spiritual rules" are ones that have been observed, both in personal spiritual practice and spiritual practice with various associated groups and teachers. These rules universally govern any spiritual practice, and appear to be in effect whether you know them or not. Unlike ethics and morals, which change with culture and time, these spiritual rules appear to have remained the same throughout time, unchanging, like physical and scientific rules.

The rules in the following section are adapted from *Rules of the Road*, as created by George Dew, co-founder of the Church of Seven Arrows. There are two major rules, which are common to most spiritual practices, along with some minor rules that are specific to our form of magickal practice.

Two Major Rules

These two rules will probably sound familiar, as they appear in most major religions and spiritual practices, most probably because they are common-sense and apply not just to spiritual practice, but to life as well.

First Rule: Golden Rule or Law of Karma
This first rule is literally a "golden oldie":

What you do to the environment or to other beings in the environment brings similar effects back to you in your life.

    Often recognized as the Golden Rule or the Law of Karma, this rule tops the list because it reminds all spiritual practitioners of potential unwanted "rebound" or side effects. As your spiritual power, focus, and abilities grow, this rule will have an ever-greater impact on your life unless you exercise caution. The Universe responds more strongly and powerfully to those with focus, power, and ability.

    Note: As humanity moves further in the Aquarian Age, many spiritual practitioners have seen more effects from this rule occur faster. In the past, effects of this rule that often took lifetimes to manifest now occur in minutes, days, weeks, or months. In this particular time in Earth's history, karma seems to operate under a "pay as you go" system. Simply stated, expect the effects of the Law of Karma to occur quickly.

Second Rule: The Judgment of "Good and Bad" According to the Universe
    This second rule adds clarity and detail to the first rule described previously:

If you are unsure whether your acts are "good or bad"-- that is, whether those acts are in keeping with universal laws on this planet—the Universe will reflect its judgment back to you quickly, according to the "pay as you go" Law of Karma.

    This law holds as true for individuals as it does for entire communities, states, nations, or other organized groups. If you are still unsure of the feedback you receive from the Universe, check areas such as your level of health, the soundness of social relationships, your prosperity or lack of, sufficiency of various needs in life, and even your "luck" with appliances and machines. If your luck appears to be consistently poor, then you are probably acting contrary to universal governing laws, regardless of your intentions. The Universe cares about what you do more than what you intend.

Additional Detailed Rules

The following rules offer more detailed standards by which to measure your acts or the acts of others to determine whether these acts are in accordance with universal laws.

- Do nothing that will harm another being unless you are willing to suffer similar or greater harm. What the Universe considers "harm" may be different than what you consider harm.
- Do not bind another being unless you are willing to be similarly bound. An example of binding someone is doing acts in attempt to coerce a specific other person to love you. There is no problem with attracting your soul mate into your life, but doing acts that attempt to coerce a specific other person to love you is a type of binding.
- Never use your spiritual abilities in vain, to show off, or to boost your pride. Using your spiritual abilities from a place of pride usually causes the Universe to bring instant backlash into your life.
- If you choose to charge money or barter for using your spiritual abilities in the service of others, avoid charging extremely high prices. Charge prices for using methods comparable to other professionals, such as an attorney or accountant.
- Never use any spiritual word, chant, litany, or similar "device" unless you are confident in your understanding of its methods, intents, and effects.
- When undertaking a major spiritual operation—one that will require significant effort or attempts to create a major effect in the world—use divination to determine whether you can safely benefit from such

15

an operation, and to discover the obstacles you must overcome. Divination methods such as pendulum readings, channeling, meditation, and question circles (to name a few) can reveal hidden factors of which you may be unaware.

- In any spiritual endeavor, take your time, think it through, and do it right!

The good news is that you can still cast a love spell and do love rituals. The ones we teach in this book won't get you in trouble with the Universe, yet will still allow you to attract the soul mate of your dreams. While you can't cast a spell to make a specific person fall for you, you can cast a spell to bring a partner of your dreams into your life (which may end up to be the same person, or be better than the person you've had your eye on).

The Ingredients of Love Magick

"Love is the only sane and satisfactory answer to the problem of human existence."
~Erich Fromm

Valentine's Day is often thought of as the day of love. Valentine was actually a bishop during the reign of Roman Emperor Claudius II and is known as the patron saint of all lovers. That title stems from the fact that he continued to perform marriage ceremonies for young Roman couples after Claudius banned marriages. Claudius believed that men who were married made poor soldiers, and he needed more good soldiers. Most historians state that Valentine was actually executed by the Romans on February 14th, which is why this date was chosen as a day for lovers in his honor.

Love and Magic

The energy surrounding Valentine's Day makes it the perfect time to use magick to attract love to your life. For example, the use of a love talisman, which we'll introduce later in the book in more detail, is an ideal way to attract love. One of the talismans we'll talk about has a vial with a stopper that you can fill with such ingredients as dried Lavender and Yarrow, both of which are known for their abilities to attract love. Whether you want to find your soul mate or just fill your life with love, this type of vial necklace is a powerful yet discreet amulet that keeps love close to your heart!

Before we dive into the ins and outs of how to do the seven love rituals in this book, let's talk a little bit about love in general. Many people inquire about using a love spell to make a particular person fall in love with them or to mend a broken relationship by having a partner who has left return to them. Still others want to make someone in another love relationship leave that relationship and fall in love with them instead. The problem with using magick in any of these situations is that it breaks the Rules of the Road, which are the fundamental rules that govern magickal practice. Breaking these rules can cause major backlash. Love spells of this nature don't work because they break the rule that says:

Don't bind another being unless you are willing to be likewise bound. This applies to many love spells and some kinds of healing rituals.

Another way to think about it is in terms of the Golden Rule. Don't do unto others what you would not want done to you. Think about this: would you want someone that you don't really love to bind you and make you fall in love with them? Probably not. The same holds true in your situation. If the person of your dreams doesn't love you, then binding him or her with a love spell may cause him or her to pay attention to you in the short term, but the long-term backlash could get ugly. The problem is that you'll have a hard time predicting what kind of karmic backlash would result from this kind of spell. So, before we get into using magick to attract love to your life, make sure you thoroughly understand the Rules of the Road that govern magickal practice as presented in the previous section.

Love Magick Appetizer Recipes

Appetizers: Gain Answers to Get Started

Question Circles: Get the Answers You Need for Your Love Life

Ask Spirit of Owl: Remove Hidden Blockages to Love

"I definitely had my doubts about getting actual useful information from 'unseen Spirits.' After all I was unsure whether I would be able to tell whether I was hearing my own thoughts or actually receiving information from the Universe. What made me a believer was the fact that the information I got was nothing like I would ever come up with."
~ Fred W., Hopland, CA

[this page intentionally left blank]

Question Circles: Get the Answers You Need for Your Love Life

"Love is the magickian that pulls man out of his own hat."
~Ben Hecht

Time Required: Sixty Minutes

Not sure why your love life isn't all that you want it to be? Use this Question Circle Recipe to get the answers you need about your life ... the who, what, where, why and how! Ask Spirit Guides to provide the answers you need about your love life!

Ingredients
- 1 Sun Yellow (bright yellow) candle, preferably in glass – easily available at your grocery store
- wooden or paper matches (no lighters)
- a compass to help you locate cardinal directions (North, South, East, West)
- your favorite pen and pad of paper

21

- an open space, five or ten feet in diameter, in which you can set up your circle

Recipe Directions

1. Use your compass outside to locate the four cardinal directions (compasses don't work well inside so use it outside).

2. Gather a Sun Yellow candle that can easily be carried from place to place, paper or wooden matches, a pen, and paper.

3. Plot out an open space of five to ten feet in diameter and mentally mark the cardinal directions of North, South, East and West.

4. Sit in the South facing North with your Sun Candle in front of you. Light the candle with wooden or paper matches and hold your hands around the flame while saying in a voice of command:

Child of Wonder
Child of Flame
Nourish My Spirit and
Protect My Aim.

5. Sit in the center of the circle facing East, and write two to three questions that you most want answered about your love life. These questions might be something like, "What is keeping me from attracting my soul mate?" or "What steps do I need to take to attract the love of my life?" Write down no more than three questions since Spirit Guides will answer almost all questions with voluminous answers.

6. Sit and contemplate your question for three to five minutes, letting the question sit in your mind without

trying to answer it. Just focus on the questions.

7. Get up and move to the East perimeter of the circle carrying your Sun Yellow candle and your paper and pen with you. Sit in this area facing East, and set the candle down in front of you.

8. Ask your question aloud to the East. Be prepared for a flurry of information. The information usually comes faster than you can write it. Write until the flow of information stops and then send your thanks out in that direction. If you have more than one question, then repeat the same process with your second question. Do the same with your third question.

9. Get up and move in a clockwise direction to the next direction—sit in the South facing South—and repeat the process as outlined in steps seven and eight.

10. Continue this process going around the circle to the West and North. Then go back to the center of the circle facing East again and sit there.

11. Send your thanks out all the way around the circle and blow out your sun candle.

How to Use the Results of Your Recipe

You now have papers full of information. Each direction will have given you different types of information. For instance, the East will give you information about communication, planning, and ideas. The South will give you guidance on action steps, will power, energy, and desire. The West will give you feelings and spiritual guidance, while the North will give you practical advice. Use the information that is immediately helpful and relevant for you, and store the rest in a safe place for later use.

[this page intentionally left blank]

Ask Spirit of Owl: Remove Hidden Blockages to Love

"Your task is not to seek for love, but merely to seek and find all the barriers within yourself that you have built against it."
~Rumi

Time Required: Forty-Five Minutes

If you have been unsuccessfully attracting a certain kind of person into your life for a long time, then you may be running into hidden or subconscious blockages. One way to discover how you might be getting in your own way with these blockages is to consult the Spirit of Owl, the seer of unseen things. The Owl totem has all of the best qualities of physical owls: they can see extremely well, can hear extremely well, can turn their heads 180 degrees (the equivalent of having eyes in the back of their heads), are wise, and are excellent hunters. If you have a blind spot with regard to love and relationships, the Spirit of Owl may be

25

able to help you uncover and discover that blockage. Once discovered, you can go to work discarding that barrier to love from your life.

Ingredients
- A quiet place free from distractions
- Paper and pen optional to write down discoveries throughout the day

Recipe Directions
1. Say aloud or in your mind, "Spirit of Owl, I request your help."

2. Wait a few moments until you feel the presence of Owl (no more than a few seconds). Even if you are not able to feel the presence of the Spirit of Owl at this point, just know that Owl always appears when someone requests their presence and help.

3. State your request. For instance, if you need help seeing why you keep having negative love relationships, you might say, "Owl, please come with me today and show me what is causing these negative relationships in my life. Please show me in a way that I can clearly understand. Thank you in advance for your help." Appreciation is very important to this process. Appreciation before, during, and after the process is one of the best ways to honor a Spirit guide such as the Spirit of Owl.

4. Keep an open mind to what Owl will show you. Owl will ride with you on your shoulder, whispering in your ear, giving you knowing and understanding where before you had only blindness and confusion.

How to Use the Results of Your Recipe
Owl may bring up old memories, send you a phrase from the mouth of a stranger or bring a chance meeting with

another person. Owl will use any and every device to help you see. If at the end of the stated period of time, a day in the above example, you still don't understand what Owl is showing you, ask again the next day. Each day Owl will make it more obvious to you. Each time you gain a new insight or understanding, thank Owl for the help. Remember that Owl penetrates secrets and veils, and can show you anything you wish to know. All you have to do is ask! Sometimes just being aware of what has been blocking your perfect love from reaching you is enough for you to tear down those barriers. Other times your new insights will give you answers on how to increase the energetic flow for you to attract your perfect love.

[this page intentionally left blank]

Love Magick Main Course Recipes

Main Courses: Heat Up Your Love Life

Directors and Limiters: Cook Up True Love

Sun Candle: Light Up Your Love Life

Add a Talisman: Carry Love Magick Everywhere You Go

"I have always wanted to try my hand at love magick but didn't want to be obvious about it until I had a chance to see if it would work or not. I did all three rituals—Directors and Limiters, Sun Candle, and Talisman—in sequence. Keeping my hands and my mind busy with these simple rituals does the same thing for me as cooking does. Both help me stay occupied until the 'watched pot' boils, so to speak. Color me surprised when a new love appeared in my life seven months later. I guess cooking up an entree in the kitchen and cooking up a little love magick have a lot in common. Both are fun and both have wonderfully delicious results!"
~ Jerry A., Richmond, VA

[this page intentionally left blank]

Directors and Limiters: Cook Up True Love

"A joyful heart is the inevitable result of a heart burning with love."
~Mother Teresa

Time Required: Ninety Minutes

The starting point of any love magick—be it potion, spell, mantra, or ritual—is to define what you want in very clear terms. The Universe is a very literal interpreter of your requests, so you want to be very clear about what you want to attract and what you don't want to attract in your future soul mate. We call these specifications "Directors and Limiters." Directors and limiters define what any love spell, potion, ritual, talisman, or technique will do (directors) and won't do (limiters). Think of them as your karmic safety net.

Ingredients
- Paper and pen
- Your thinking cap

- A quiet place free of distractions to get in touch with your inner guidance

Recipe Directions

1. Sit in a quiet comfortable space free of distractions and envision the perfect love match for you.

2. Pay attention to details as you envision this other person without attaching a physical face or body to the image.

3. Notice the character traits of this person, the values they hold, their behaviors, type of lifestyle they lead, their social status, age, and anything else that you are looking for in a love partner.

4. Begin to write down the characteristics that you find attractive in this person.

5. After you have a list going, divide it into two sections. One for Directors that will be very specific as to the type of person you want to attract to your life, but that will not bind any specific person. And one for Limiters. In your list of Directors, allow room for the Universe to work by stating ranges when you can instead of specific numbers (e.g., with age or dollars). An example of some Directors could include:
   - is between the ages of 30 and 40
   - lives within 100 miles of you
   - has a steady job and earns between $x and $y
   - shares similar interests as you (you might want to get specific here)
   - has a certain kind of personality (intellectual, witty, quiet, outgoing...)
   - has any other desired characteristics (well-groomed, long hair, particular race...)

6. In your list of Limiters write down everything that is important to you NOT to be included in this person's character or in the relationship. An example of some Limiters could include:

- does not have any pre-existing health issues
- does not have any children from previous marriages
- any other limiters you do not want to bring into a new relationship (i.e. – does not drink alcohol or use drugs, is not a violent person, has no criminal past....)

How to Use the Results of Your Recipe

You obviously can't come up with everything to put on your Directors and Limiters list, so focus on the most important factors for you. The more specific your lists are the more force it will take to bring a person having all those characteristics into your life. If you already have a lot of resistance in the love department start with a more generalized list with fewer demands. As your spell or ritual begins bringing potential partners into your life, you can then go back and tweak the list until the exact right person shows up in your life. This step in magickally attracting your perfect partner is crucial, so give some careful thought to the type of person you want to attract and sit down to write out your Directors and Limiters. Then you'll be ready to move on to using this list to attract your perfect mate.

[this page intentionally left blank]

Sun Candle: Light Up Your Love Life

"Love must be as much a light, as it is a flame."
~Henry David Thoreau

Time Required: Forty-Five Minutes

A Sun Candle is one of the easiest magickal tools to begin using with spells. Sun Yellow, which is a pure bright yellow color with no oranges tones, is a fire energy color on the spiritual level that represents life force, nourishment of Spirit, and can help you overcome sluggish emotional states. It is also a very safe fire element color to use for beginners. With this ritual, you will be launching your love spell and sending out your completed list of Directors and Limiters to the Universe and adding fire energy into the energetic matrix.

Ingredients
- Sun Yellow Candle (pure yellow without orange overtones and preferably unscented)

- Wooden or paper matches (do not use a lighter)
- Plate to safely set the candle on
- Completed list of Directors and Limiters
- Compass if needed to find the cardinal direction South

Recipe Directions

1. Charge the Sun Candle, which means to program it, to enhance your list to begin the process of giving your Directors and Limiters extra power with the Sun Candle. To charge the candle:
   - Stand or sit in the South facing North with the Sun Candle in front of you.
   - Light the candle using wooden or paper matches (do NOT use a lighter).
   - Wait until the candle flame is steady and tall.
   - Hold your hands up to and around the flame, focusing your attention on the candle and flame.

   Say the charge verse below in a voice of command:

   Child of Wonder
   Child of Flame
   Nourish My Spirit
   And Protect My Aim.

2. Use this charged Sun Candle to launch your simple love spell by placing your list of Directors and Limiters under the Sun Candle on a plate.

3. Leave the candle burning in the room for at least 30 minutes (be sure the candle is on a protected surface such as a plate and is not a fire hazard). This will "launch" your spell into the Universe so it can begin attracting your desired love.

4. At the end of 30 minutes or when you feel ready, blow out the flame (don't snuff it).

5. Spend a moment or two in the area to see if you can detect a difference in the level and quality of energy. The area should feel lighter, more harmonious, and possibly more energized.

How to Use the Results of Your Recipe

You can also repeat this process every day to direct power and force into the spell matrix. For some people, performing this operation everyday gives them the feeling of doing something and helps them resist the urge to "do." That will get in the way of the Universe doing its job. This is the time to let go and trust that you have done your part so you can allow the magick to work and deliver to you that which you desire.

[this page intentionally left blank]

Add a Talisman: Carry Love Magick Everywhere You Go

Time Required: Forty-Five Minutes

Sometimes love magick works better when we psychically connect a talisman of some kind, such as a necklace or pendant or ring, to the spell. This connection to something physical helps many people to feel the manifestation becoming a reality. Wearing a talisman, or carrying one around, also reminds you that you are conducting a magickal act. The talisman also reminds you of the various magickal exercises in which you are engaged, such as seeing the good in each person, and working with the Sun Candle daily. To key or connect a talisman to your love magick, first you have to choose a talisman. Take some time to think about something that speaks to you of the love you seek. You may want to find a small stoppered bottle or vial on a chain. Put a tiny version of your Directors and Limiters in the bottle, and wear the chain and pendant daily. You could also put dried herbs that are known to attract love. Other people like to use stones, such as hematite or rose quartz, which can be carried in the pocket. Yet others choose angel figurines or animal totems. Choose whatever speaks to you. Once you have selected a talisman, you will need to connect it to the spell you have created. Here's the recipe for connecting your talisman to your love spell launched in the previous section.

Ingredients

- The talisman that you have selected
- The setup with Sun Candle, plate, and list of Directors and Limiters used when launching your spell

Recipe Directions

1. You can do this the first time you launch your spell or during any of the subsequent times you perform the operation adding in more energetic force.

2. Place your talisman on the plate on top of the list of your Directors and Limiters (next to the Sun Candle).

3. Leave the talisman there each time you light and burn the Sun Candle.

4. Doing this ritual repeatedly for several days (at least three to seven days) will connect your talisman to your love magick.

5. After the talisman has been connected (or "keyed") you can start wearing or carrying it around.

How to Use the Results of Your Recipe

Every time you notice your talisman, remember to find the good in others. Think back on your Directors and

Limiters. Remain open to the unexpected. The energy you project from this type of mindset will continue to "key" the talisman daily even as you begin to use it.

[this page intentionally left blank]

Love Magick Dessert Recipes

Desserts – Whipped Cream with a Cherry on Top!

Sweet Endings: Unlock Your Heart and Stay Open to Love

The Universal Cherry on Top: Let the Universe Lead Your Heart

"Affirmations, mandalas, meditations, dream boards... I've done them all. To say I was pessimistic about the Universe delivering my love wishes to is an understatement. I was pleasantly surprised when the exercises helped me gain faith in the goodness and reliability of the Universe in baby steps. The love I was seeking was really just a few baby steps away. Those of us who are impatient, like me, really can benefit from these simple love magick rituals, which teach us to walk before we run!"
~ Janice P., Bismarck, ND

[this page intentionally left blank]

Sweet Endings: Unlock Your Heart and Stay Open to Love

"Love unlocks doors and opens windows that weren't even there before."
~Mignon McLaughlin

Time Required: Thirty Minutes

The Universe is always ready to deliver what we want and that includes the perfect love relationship. In any type of manifestation, however, we often get in our own way and block it from coming to us. Once we have put out to the Universe what we want, our job is to get out of the way and let the Universe deliver. In the case of a magickally-inspired relationship, often happens that neither party was "expecting" to find love in the place they discovered it. For instance, one woman used some love magic, and then expectantly waited for a stranger to visit from across the country—just so she could fall in love with that stranger. Instead, she finds herself falling in love with the person who has lived in the same neighborhood for more than a decade. Or maybe two rivaling lawyers wrangling over a court case

45

rife with animosity discover love over drinks after the case is over.

The moral of the story is to keep an open mind as to where you will find love—and with whom. You can give the Universe the room to work and open the energetic flow of love to come into your life by working on changing your perspective and opening your mind.

There is a magickal law that says, "The level of your being attracts the level of your life." This means that you will only attract a love that is a match for you. If you project negativity then that is what you will attract. This exercise will help you focus on staying positive. This helps you remain open to where, when, and whom the Universe will bring into your life as your perfect mate. Keeping an open and positive outlook also helps you move through life much more joyfully, enjoying people a great deal more. Once you widen your perspective, you'll be able to begin seeing love in a variety of places, not just the usual places you look. In addition, you may find that someone you might have previously avoided for one reason or another can actually have good traits.

Ingredients
- Your favorite pen and notepad
- An open mind
- A willingness to experiment with non-judgment
- The capacity to have a positive outlook

Recipe Directions
1. Sit in a comfortable position with your pen and notepad within reach. Take a few moments to quiet your mind, do some deliberate breathing, or use any other technique to calm your mind, body, and Spirit.

2. Now pick up your pen and pad, and jot down five to seven names of people with whom you come into regular contact. Don't think about this process, simply jot down the first names that come to you.

3. Concentrating on one person at a time from your list, seek to find at least one positive attribute for each person. Jot down a that positive aspect next to the person's name. If negative impressions start coming into your mind about that person, stop your thoughts and refocus looking for a positive.

4. Don't necessarily look at each person as a potential mate, just use this time to practice looking for the positive aspects in others, projecting positive energies, and being open to changing perspectives.

5. If you come across someone that you really are having trouble finding something positive about, pick something small such as the fact that they have nice hair, straight teeth, or don't have body odor. Simply find one positive characteristic about each person, no matter how small or insignificant. Then move on to the next person.

6. At the end of the day, review if this exercise helped you remain more positive about the people you met during the day. See if you have changed your attitude about people whom you previously disliked completely. Even a small shift in your attitude towards that person can bring a big shift in your level of being.

7. If you had difficulty finding positive aspects about a particular person (but did so anyway), look back and discover whether your attitude about that person shifted to a more positive outlook. If so, repeat the exercise using this person as your point of focus, and see if you can expand the number of positive characteristics about this person.

How to Use the Results of Your Recipe

If you absolutely have a strong negative reaction to a certain person and cannot find anything positive about him or her, see if you can discover the reason behind your dislike of this person. You might want to do a Question Circle or work with the Spirit of Owl to gather information about the reasons you have such an adverse reaction to this person. Gaining an understanding of how certain traits are abhorrent to you can also be valuable information and allow you to discover possible areas of growth for you to work on to raise your level of being. As your level of being increases, you may want to repeat this exercise. Notice how your reactions to all kinds of people become increasingly positive. Some people elect to do this exercise once a week to gain a spiritual boost, and to draw more love into their lives.

We do not ask you to look at something that is black and call it white. We do not ask you to see something that is not as you want it to be and pretend that it is. What we ask you to do is practice moving your gaze. Practice changing your perspective. Practice talking to different people. Practice going to new places. Practice sifting through the data for the things that feel like you want to feel and using those things to cause you to feel a familiar place. In other words, we want you to feel familiar in your joy. Familiar in your positive expectation, familiar in your knowing that all is well, because this Universe will knock itself out giving you evidence of that Well-being once you find that place. We have enjoyed this interaction immensely.

~ Abraham

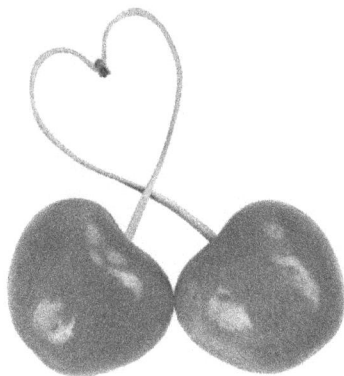

The Universal Cherry on Top: Let the Universe Lead Your Heart

"To find someone who will love you for no reason, and to shower that person with reasons, that is the ultimate happiness."
~Robert Brault

Time Required: Fifteen Minutes

Some people find it difficult to just sit back and trust that the Universe will deliver that which they have asked for. This doubt factor in your life can interfere with your openness to love. When you live in doubt, you hinder the Universe's ability to deliver. Imagine the Universe trying to deliver a package to you, but you're not home to sign for the package when your doorbell rings. This recipe on making Conscious Choices offers you another magickal operation to engage your attention so that you feel as if you are "doing something." This exercise will also help you further establish your faith and trust in the Universe. With this exercise you turn one or more small decisions over to the Universe, then follow the Universe's answers without question. Doing this exercise for at least 40 days in a row will increase your faith in the Universe's ability to guide you toward your desired goals.

Ingredients
- Willingness to experiment with trusting the Universe's guidance

Recipe Directions
1. Quiet your inner self by taking a few deep breaths.

2. Say to yourself, either aloud or silently, "I will now make a conscious choice."

3. Ask yourself a choice question, such as, "Do I choose to xxx or not?" or "Do I choose to do this or that?" (i.e. – Do I choose to go for a run or watch a movie? Do I choose to have cereal or eggs for breakfast? Do I choose to eat lunch at the diner or not? ....). Start with questions of little consequence that won't be life altering until you become comfortable with the process and establish a firm connection of trust and communication with the Universe.

4. The first answer you "hear" internally (or sometimes externally from a passing person) is what you must follow. Don't sit and think about an answer, just take the first one that pops into your head. You may not, in this recipe, avoid doing the option you have consciously chosen. That is one reason we say start with small things that won't matter a lot as to which choice you hear.

5. Repeat this exercise as many times per day as you like. The more frequently you ask the Universe for

guidance, the more you will respect the power of the Universe to understand your desires and deliver them to you.

How to Use the Results of Your Recipe

The Conscious Choice recipe is magickal because it puts you in touch with your spiritual wisdom and gives you practice on following the answers you "hear" from your spiritual self. By learning to trust your spiritual wisdom, which comes from a connection to the Universe, you will never find yourself in the wrong place. Plus, you get to practice the idea that there are no wrong decisions. Following your intentions puts you on your magickal path, and the conscious choice recipe is a perfect, simple, and subtle way to exercise your intention.

Dedicate yourself to following this recipe for at least 40 days. If you miss doing it for one day, start over at Day One. The idea of using this exercise 40 days in a row is to demonstrate your dedication to a small magickal practice as a part of your love magick. As they say, "What you pay into your practice pays you back." What you pay into the Conscious Choice recipe will pay you back in spades... and hearts!

[this page intentionally left blank]

More Magickal Resources

Kindle or Paperback on Amazon:
1. ***Witchcraft Spell Book Series:***
   - Learn How to Do Witchcraft Rituals and Spells with Your Bare Hands (Witchcraft Spell Books, Book 1)
   - Learn How to Do Witchcraft Rituals and Spells with Household Ingredients (Witchcraft Spell Books, Book 2)
   - Learn How to Do Witchcraft Rituals and Spells with Magical Tools (Witchcraft Spell Books, Book 3)
   - Witchcraft Spell Book: The Complete Guide of Witchcraft Rituals & Spells for Beginners (compilation of Books 1, 2 & 3)
2. ***Kitchen Table Magick Series***

Ebooks and Online Courses at *www.shamanschool.com*
Wand: Air Tool
Athame: Fire Tool
Chalice: Water Tool
Plate: Earth Tool
Magical Tool: Firebowl
Psychic Development
Energy Healing For Self and Others

How to Do Voodoo
Daily Rituals to Attract What You Want in Life

__Find a complete list of magickal resources on__
__https://amzn.to/3swxvPo. These resources are__
__constantly updated so check back often!__

Free Gift Offer

To thank you for purchasing this book, I'd like to give you a

100% FREE GIFT

Learn more about your free magickal gift.

Access Your Free Gift at www.shamanschool.com

Find a complete list of magickal resources on https://amzn.to/3swxvPo. These resources are constantly updated so check back often!

About G. Alan Joel

Magick means many things to different people. The form of magick taught by G. Alan Joel for more than 30 years is steeped in tribal traditions from around the world, from both modern tribal cultures and those from the past, which have been mostly passed on through oral dialog.

At the very heart of the magick that Mr. Joel teaches is the use of Universal Laws for the benefit of self, others, and even the planet. These magickal traditions can take on many forms, including simple rituals for daily use, specific spells for particular life situations, the use of simulacra (often better known as voodoo), weather working, water witching, the use of the elemental tools (Firebowl, Wand, Athame, Chalice, and Plate), magickal self-defense rituals, and more. Also included are the use of the Tarot for divination and spellwork, divination rituals of all kinds, Spirit-to-Spirit communication, exercises for psychic development, and abundant healing techniques.

Through his 30 plus years of studying, teaching, and honing his magickal practice, G. Alan Joel has helped thousands of people successfully integrate the magickal, and seemingly miraculous, into their daily lives. In fact, one of the greatest gifts Mr. Joel has offered through his teachings is the ability for his students to always find a magickal solution for life situations that often seem impossible to solve. With magick, anything is possible in the mundane world. All that is required of the practitioner is an open mind, the desire to learn, and a willingness to pay some time and effort into his or her magickal practice. One of Mr. Joel's favorite quotes is:

"What you pay into your practice pays you back!"

While many magickal traditions have fiercely guarded their secrets from the public, Mr. Joel feels that "Magick is the birthright of every planetary citizen." As such he strives to offer magickal teachings that are easily learned and inexpensive (no excessive fees to join exclusive magickal groups or ascend up the levels of learning). He also offers techniques that are usable and effective for all who are sincere in their desire to practice magick. In essence, Mr. Joel's methods teach a form of "Every Man's (and Woman's) Magick." All are welcome, his teachings are simple. yet effective, and he also offers online classes in which he helps students troubleshoot their magickal issues in an interactive setting.

Find out more about Mr. Joel's teachings here and on his website (***www.shamanschool.com***) where magickal offerings are updated on a regular basis.

Mr. Joel augments this magickal knowledge and teaching with 30 years of practice as Doctor of Chinese Medicine, including a deep understanding of herbology and acupuncture. His understanding of the healing arts deepens the magickal knowledge he teaches, as magickal healing is a major aspect of his teachings. Mr. Joel believes that while there is clearly a time and place for Western Medicine, magickal and Eastern healing techniques can be harmoniously blended in to offer people many choices for healing all types of health conditions.

About the Esoteric School of Shamanism and Magic

The Esoteric School of Shamanism and Magic was started from a desire for all people from all over the globe to be able to attend a real, if virtual, school dedicated to magick and shamanism. The aim of the Esoteric School of Shamanism and Magic is to help people create permanent, positive change in their lives through the study of esoteric magickal and shamanic knowledge. It doesn't matter what your esoteric background is, whether you started out with witchcraft, religious studies, spirituality or candle magick, we welcome you. We believe that the Truth is the same, no matter which form you practice. We delight in all manner of shamanic schools and traditions, magickal techniques and esoteric ritual. You can visit us at *www.shamanschool.com*, our blog at *http://shamanmagic.blogspot.com*, or on social media via links on our website.

[this page intentionally left blank]

[this page intentionally left blank]

[this page intentionally left blank]

[this page intentionally left blank]

www.ingramcontent.com/pod-product-compliance
Lightning Source LLC
Chambersburg PA
CBHW060704030426
42337CB00017B/2765